BE A UNICORN

& live life on the bright side

BE A UNICORN

& live life on the bright side

SARAH FORD

ILLUSTRATED BY
ANITA MANGAN

Andrews McMeel
PUBLISHING®

FOR FLORRIE

NOTES

Always read this book with a smile on your face, but not on the toilet (unicorns would never do that).

Contains explicitly happy content.

Rated PG (good for positivity guidance).

Not for non-believers.

Spread the love.

Be a unicorn. Unicorn is fearless and kind, he always tries to be positive and see the good in others, but he also loves laughter and mischief, so be on guard, as there is often a harmless prank up his sleeve.

Unicorn likes to see the funny side of things and enjoys everything he does.

He is proud to be different and full of positive energy; you will never find Unicorn standing on the sidelines. He is always the first on the dance floor and doesn't care what anyone else thinks . . . after all, music and body are made for enjoyment. Unicorn is happy in his own skin, he loves himself and everyone around him. He chooses to live in the moment and doesn't dwell on the past (that's gone), or worry about the future (who knows what that will bring).

If you live life like Unicorn then you are destined to be happy, with a full cup that overflows with glitter and goodness.

Be a unicorn, and you will make the world a more colorful, happy, and peaceful place.

UNICORN'S 10 RULES FOR A GOOD LIFE

- Be nice. It's free and easy, and if you do stuff for others it makes you feel really good inside.

- A little bit of daydreaming can be fun, but it's much better to trot up the mountain, smell the flowers, and make things happen . . . it's good to take part.

- Every day brings something good, funny, new, or exciting . . . jot it all down and remember to feel thankful.

- Know that sometimes you will make mistakes. After all, you are only a unicorn. It's not the end of the world, so be kind to yourself.

- Your time is precious, so spend it with like-minded unicorns and those who are important to you.

- Don't just chat, listen . . . there is wisdom all around if you choose to hear it.

- Make time to do nothing, and give your mind a good rest so you can be fresh as a daisy for whatever comes next.

- Cake is delicious, but unicorns cannot live by cake alone . . . eat the kale too and you will keep healthy. And if you do some exercise as well, that's even better.

- Buying and accumulating stuff will not make you happy. The best things in life really are free . . .
hugs, kisses,
sunshine, smiles,
rainbows, flowers,
and small furry
animals.

- Love yourself,
even your lumps
and bumps . . .
they are all part of
what makes you a
unique, special, and
mythical creature.

Unicorn found that
unlikely friendships
could bring great joy.

Unicorn enjoyed
dressing for dinner;
today he was Morrissey,
but tomorrow he had big
plans for Frida Kahlo.

Unicorn thought it was better to look at the rainbow than to waste time digging for gold.

He hadn't bathed for days, but Unicorn still smelled of roses.

Unicorn thought,
"Why walk when
you can skip?"

Unicorn found
stroking the cat's ears
really therapeutic.

Unicorn had spent a bit too
long smelling the lavender.

Unicorn loved to feel
the rain on his cheeks.

Unicorn was feeling
thankful . . . he had
avoided the poop.

On a Wednesday,
Unicorn just
went around
complimenting
everyone.

When stressed,
Unicorn put on loud
music and made a
warm casserole.

Someone had told
Unicorn that dark
chocolate was good
for his heart.

Unicorn tried really hard not to judge a book by its cover.

Being different could
be hard, but Unicorn
embraced it.

He had slept for eight hours, and Unicorn could most definitely smell the coffee.

Life had given Unicorn
lemons, so he decided to
squeeze them on his hair.

Unicorn found the
biggest challenge
with meditating was
clearing his mind of
happy thoughts.

Unicorn found his smile
was quite infectious.

Unicorn chose to
buy the shoes.

It might have been
a weed, but Unicorn
thought it was
beautiful.

The upside of his roots
showing was a trip to the
salon for Friday fizz.

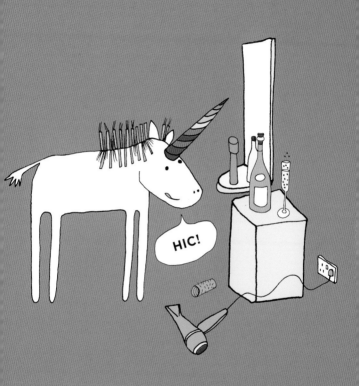

Being an ostrich
just didn't work
for Unicorn.

Unicorn enjoyed
the small things.

Unicorn decided to look
at the bigger picture.

Unicorn laughed
so much at his own
joke that he made a
small puddle.

Today, Unicorn
wanted to make hay.

Unicorn had a
"can-do" attitude.

On bad days, Unicorn felt
sure that there would be
something better just
around the corner.

Unicorn danced like there
was no one looking.

Unicorn decided to
wear the bikini.

With his shades on,
Unicorn was feeling
invincible.

While concentrating
on his breathing
techniques, Unicorn
let out a small toot.

Unicorn enjoyed the
wind in his hair.

Unicorn liked sharing, except
when it came to his potato chips.

Unicorn definitely
got his money's worth
out of his friends-and-
family deal.

Unicorn thought he
was good enough.

Unicorn's new exercise
class made him come alive.

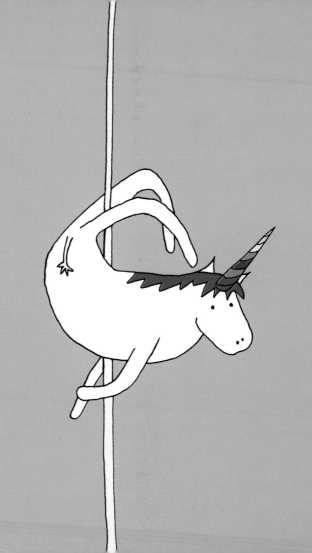

Unicorn hoped you could never have too much love.

Unicorn decided it
was much better to
give than to receive.

On wet days, Unicorn
did his coloring.

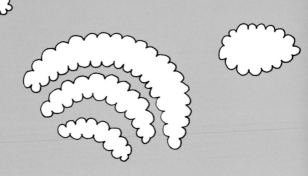

Watching clouds made
Unicorn feel really happy.

Unicorn chose to jump
in the puddles.

Unicorn found that whenever one door shut, another one opened.

The End . . . Now trot
off and be a unicorn.

Be a Unicorn

Andrews McMeel Publishing
a division of Andrews McMeel Universal
1130 Walnut Street, Kansas City, Missouri 64106

www.andrewsmcmeel.com

17 18 19 20 21   10 9 8 7 6 5 4 3 2 1

ISBN: 978-1-4494-9117-8

Library of Congress Control Number: 2017943542

Editor: Melissa Rhodes
Art Director: Diane Marsh
Production Editor: David Shaw
Production Manager: Carol Coe

Be a Unicorn was first published in Great Britain in 2017 by
Spruce, a division of Octopus Publishing Group Ltd.

Attention: Schools and Businesses
Andrews McMeel books are available at
quantity discounts with bulk purchase for
educational, business, or sales promotional use.
For information, please e-mail the Andrews
McMeel Publishing Special Sales Department:
specialsales@amuniversal.com.